Eritis Mihi Testes

Fr. Eugene Azorji

En Route Books and Media, LLC
Saint Louis, MO

⊕ENROUTE
Make the time

En Route Books and Media, LLC
5705 Rhodes Avenue
St. Louis, MO 63109

Contact us at **contactus@enroutebooksandmedia.com**

Cover Credit: Sebastian Mahfood

Copyright 2024 Eugene Azorji

ISBN-13: 979-8-88870-145-4
Library of Congress Control Number: 2024933762

All rights reserved. No part of this book may be reproduced, stored in a retrieval system, or transmitted in any form, or by any means, electronic, mechanical, photocopying, or otherwise, without the prior written permission of the author.

Dedication

This book is dedicated to
the late Sister Evangeline Enyi, HHCJ

Gratitude

I would like to thank the following in this small essay "**ERITIS MIHI TESTES**": Most Reverend Edward Burns, the Bishop of Dallas, and the auxiliary Bishop Gregory Kelly, who have assigned me to the Holy Trinity Seminary as the Spiritual director. I have enjoyed working with them and under them for over 15 years. I would like to thank **the rector** and staff of the Holy Trinity Seminary, especially Rev. Vincent Anyama, for his fraternal leadership at HTS. I thank Fr. Paul Bechter for his wonderful feedback. For all the students of HTS, I appreciate your prayers and support. May God bless your vocation and enrich you with faith and love to bear witness to the gospel.

Contents

Dedication i
Gratitude iii
Preface vii
Chapter 1: You Will Be My Witnesses 1
Chapter 2: History of False Witnesses 11
Chapter 3: Bearing Witness by Evangelizing the Cultures 17
Chapter 4: Unfinished Business of Inculturation in the Church Universal 29
Chapter 5: False Witnesses Today 35
Chapter 6: Recommendations 41
Conclusion 47
Works Consulted or Referenced 49

Preface

The audience I have in mind in writing this essay is composed of the ordinary folks (*oi poloi*) in the pews. I chose this audience for several reasons. Theology as a science of God is complicated and filled with debates and arguments that run through philosophy and social sciences. Ordinary people are not interested in those arguments. They are interested in the fundamentals of faith and the bottom line of all the debates that have erupted from the early centuries till date.

Ordinary people are preoccupied with day-to-day activities of how to make "ends meet" and how to provide food on the table. They are not concerned about rigorous search into the meaning of Karl Rahner's "transcendental anthropology," Karl Barth's "dialectics of the word of God," Rudolf Bultmann's "demythologization," or Friedrich Nietzsche's proposals of the possible "death of God theology." They simply want to pray and believe and obey.

Theologians who spend sleepless hours at night trying to figure out the positions of their colleagues on the right, left, or center end up with protracted debates that lead to more complicated obscurity. Such an endeavor is only good for the great academics in the Universities.

One of my students who is now a priest once remarked, "Fr., you know we learned a lot from the seminary, but I don't remember where my class notes are anymore." This means that this priest is now dealing with the ordinary folks in the pew who do not need "hylomorphic theories" but a simple explanation of the articles of Faith. These are the kinds of folks I have in mind in putting this essay together.

The questions that interest these kinds of folks are as follows: How was the life of the early Christians? How did they love each other. How did they organize themselves? What was their belief system? The reason is that responses to these questions help ordinary folks see continuity between the way of life of the first Christians and their own way of life.

The early Christians were credible because most of them died proclaiming the gospel, they were authentic because they practiced what they preached, they were truthful because they knew that truth is personified in Jesus of Nazareth. They were reasonable and responsible because every action of theirs had a consequence as in the case Ananias and Saphira in the Acts of the Apostles.

So, I am saying to myself, why can't Christians of the 21st century live like the Christians of the first two centuries? Why are Christians of our century preoccupied with the "fault-finding mission" of who is right or wrong, and who is left or right, to such an extent that we are deeply separated by "ideologies." This is my concern. And I guess, if you're reading this book, it is your concern, too.

Chapter 1
You Will Be My Witnesses

This statement "You will be my witnesses" is taken from the Acts of the Apostles 1:6-8 in preparation for the Ascension of Jesus. In other words, it is the departure speech of Jesus addressed to the first Christian community in Jerusalem.

The members of this first Christian community include Peter and John and James and Andrew, Philip and Thomas, Bartholomew and Matthew, James' son of Alphaeus, Simon the Zealot and Judas son of James, some women, Mary, the mother of Jesus, and his brothers. For historical purposes, these were the original members of the church before the final departure of Jesus. They were in the upper room praying and comforting each other. The names of the women were not mentioned except Mary, the mother of Jesus.

This statement came out of the context of the question asked to Jesus by the community,

> "Lord are you at this time going to restore the kingdom to Israel?" He answered them, "It is not for you to know the times or seasons that the Father

has established by his own authority. But you will receive power when the Holy Spirit comes upon you, and you will be my witnesses in Jerusalem, throughout Judea and Samaria, and to the ends of the earth. (Acts 1:6-8)

It is curious to know that the first Christian community had no power of their own until they were empowered by the Holy Spirit to start a church. It is very interesting to note that it is only after Pentecost that the first community was empowered to bear witness to what its members had seen and heard as disciples of Jesus of Nazareth. Why is it so? Because the events of the resurrection needed to be completed with the events of the ascension and Pentecost.

Chronologically, Pentecost is the accepted birthday of the Church when the first Christian community was empowered to bear witness authoritatively to the risen and ascended Christ. The first Christian community was called to bear witness to the risen and ascended Jesus of Nazareth through the power of the Holy Spirit and not through its own power or opinion. Was this power given to them collectively or individually? The scripture does not say, but since the question was directed by the whole community to Jesus, He had to answer them collectively. This meant they were to operate collectively through the Holy Spirit to witness to the truth about the life, experience, death, resurrection, and ascension of Jesus of Nazareth.

So, the church came to be born, not by way of debate among members of the early Christian community, but by living out the Christian experience in the Trinitarian way, that is, "In the name of the Father, and of the son, and of the Holy Spirit." The Church cannot operate effectively outside this trinitarian dictum. It is through the Father that the Universe came into being, and through the Son that the universe is redeemed and saved, and through the Holy Spirit that believers are empowered to bear witness to the Son in the Father: An incredible act of faith indeed!

The first empirical evidence of the risen and ascended Jesus is the birth of the Church as we see it today in so many denominations spread throughout the world. This fulfills what Jesus said before he ascended: "You will be my witnesses throughout Judea, and Samaria, and to the ends of the earth." In a way of paradox, the mission that the Church inherited from Jesus of Nazareth is yet incomplete though he instructed his disciples to go out and baptize whoever believes in him. But there are more un-believers in the world today than there were in the time of Jesus. There are more atheists, agnostics, pagans, polytheists, inactive Christians, and people who are outrightly indifferent to any religious beliefs today than in the time of Jesus.

The Early community of Christians had a strong feeling and faith in Jesus of Nazareth; they understood the essentials of Christian life. Without the lists of the written creed before them, they knew that "to love God and neighbor" was important, and they also knew that one must go extra miles to love "your enemies and pray for those who hate you." It seems to me that our generation and many of our Catholics do not understand the meaning of "Eritis mihi Testes," which translates as "You will be my witnesses" (Acts.1:8). "Whoever loves is a Christian," says Joseph Cardinal Ratzinger in his book, *Credo Today* (p. 9). I guess a witness to Jesus' love must share and possess love in himself and give it to others. A useful witness in any form of civil or criminal trial must be credible, authentic, responsible, reasonable, knowledgeable, truthful, and good. An un-useful witness may find he lacks credibility when being false, fake, irresponsible, unreasonable, lacking in knowledge, deceitful, and bad.

If Jesus of Nazareth assured the Christian community that they would be empowered by the Holy Spirit to bear witness to the truth about him and his work on earth, has that power ceased to exist? or is the church overwhelmed by the evils of secularism and relativism in the world.? I believe that the church as a community of believers has some questions to answer today on a personal basis as witnesses of the gospel to the world. Are we doing enough, or is it that what we're doing is not good enough to make a difference to the world today? Are we surrendering to the voice of the world? These questions are real and existential. The first early Christian community was **credible** because its members literally bore witness with their own lives. They were in touch with the powerful experience of the resurrection and ascension of Jesus of Nazareth. They had fresh contact with how Jesus performed miracles. They knew exactly how their Lord and Master operated. They were able to replicate the words and actions of their master after he had gone.

The classical example is the healing of the cripple at the temple after the Pentecost experience. Peter was humble enough to proclaim, "Silver or gold I don't have, but in the name of Jesus be healed" (Acts 3:6), and that was what happened. The lives the first Christian community lived were of togetherness of mind and purpose. Their personal lives were a testimony of the resurrected Jesus. They shared what they had and had personal touch with the individual needs of their members. They practiced what they preached and showed in practical terms the true meaning of AGAPE-love with sacrifice. The lives and actions of the first early Christian community were **authentic** because they lived in communion with the risen Lord and had one mission, one vision, one goal—to proclaim Jesus crucified.

There was no guile or pretense in their personal lives, and anyone who was found corrupt was removed from the community. The case of Ananias and Saphira is a classic example of the removal of a couple of bad apples from the church. Overall, then, members of the first Christian community lived holy lives and wished one another the same life of sanctity. There were no double lives, and one was either an authentic Christian or not a Christian at all.

The simple philosophy that informed the first early Christians was **reasonable** enough that they did not engage in sophisticated theories of "essence" and "existence" but simply preached Jesus crucified, died, risen, and ascended into heaven. With this background, they converted thousands in a few days. They touched lives, performed miracles, and faced persecution.

The first Christian community was very **responsible** in their respective functions. They were not preoccupied with "who the greatest among them" would be because Jesus had settled the matter on the road to Jerusalem and a second time while he was preaching there: "Whoever seeks to be greatest among you must resolve to be a servant for all" (Matthew 20:26-28, 23:11). They were all agreed on the leadership role of the first pope, Peter. His testimony after the ascension was a valid proof of his leadership role and the fulfilment of the Petrine office to be the "servant of the servants of the Lord."

They maintained this tradition 2000 years ago and handed it over to our present generation. The first early Christian community did not include among its members sophisticated folks with higher education, but ordinary men and women from the periphery of society. They were **knowledgeable** enough, though, to bear witness to the risen Lord by their actions and words and, most importantly, by their daily lives. They bore witness by their simplicity of life, by their living in communion with one another, and by their sharing and breaking of bread together, acts of *koinonia*.

The first early Christian community was **truthful** to their faith. They were faithful to their calling to discipleship, and they made an incredible impression on their followers to the point that they were called "saints," that is, those set apart for the sake of building a special kingdom here on earth for Christ. For the first community of Christians, the truth is the person of Jesus of Nazareth. Truth is not opinion or philosophy or even ideology that is current within a certain epoch. It is a person. The first century father of the Church, St. Justin the Martyr, wrote in his First Apology that behind every seed of truth is Jesus of Nazareth. This idea was prevalent in the first two centuries of Christianity. The disciples believed in the saying of Jesus, "I am the way, the truth, and the life" (John 14:6).

Concerning Philip and Thomas' little faith, Jesus was able to convince them by saying to them, "Whoever has seen me, has seen the Father…. and I and the father are one" (John 14:9), and they believed him entirely. If you ask an ordinary Christian of our generation what he or she understands to be the truth, the response will likely be, "It all depends on what type of truth?" In the early days of Christianity, this was not the case. Today, truth has been relativized to fit the cultures and nuances of our so-called western civilization. Ratzinger challenged our generation by explaining that our "practicing Christian love in the same way as Christ means that we are good to some one who needs our kindness, even if we do not like him. It means committing ourselves to the way of Jesus Christ and thus bringing about something like a Copernican revolution in our own lives." This means dying in ourselves so that others may live. Is this possible today?

There are wars going on in the world today, just for selfish reasons. When people consider themselves to be the center of gravity, they arrogate to themselves god-like power. But when we as the church focus on God as the center of our lives, we practice the agape type of love. As Pope Benedict XVI reminded us, "Being a Christian means having love. That is unbelievably difficult and at the same time, incredibly simple. Yet however difficult it may be in many respects, discovering this is still a profoundly liberating experience." The Early Christians knew this principle of Love from their master, and they put it to practice, so it is no wonder almost all of them experienced martyrdom bearing witness to the gospel. How we are living out this "agape" Christian love in our own generation today has been a problem of debate and challenges.

Chapter 2
History of False Witnesses

One of the negative sides of Christianity as a religion is the rise of **false witnesses** of the gospel among the Christian community. It began around the third century as Christianity moved from the Jewish community to the Gentiles. Through a process of acculturation and adaptation, the languages of Ancient Greek and Latin began to bear heavily on the understanding of the gospel message. The Gnostics and Greek philosophers introduced syncretistic ideas to Christianity, which is what the church historian A. Harnack called the "extreme Hellenization of Christianity." (For those who would like to read more on this, cf. *Early Christian Doctrines* by J.N.D. Kelly, Harper, and Row Publishers, 1978, p. 22.)

What followed were individuals who began to deny the divinity as well as the humanity of Jesus. The "docetes" (what seems to be real but not) were those who opined that Jesus of Nazareth was only a fantasy and appearance of the power of God above, that he was not real man, but perhaps a "superman." Then came Arius, who taught that the incarnate son was created as an ordinary human being, and perhaps, "there was a time when he was not."

For over six centuries, Christianity was in turmoil to define its creed, maintain its orthodoxy and tradition, and remain credible. "But the gates of Hell did not prevail against her." Christianity was able to establish the lists of the canon of the scriptures, the tradition of the Church in the celebration of the sacraments, the defense of the early Christian doctrines, and the survival of the hierarchical church. Church historians have written books upon books on the details of the development of the Christian faith from the Apostolic times to the present, and false witnesses and teachers continue to abound in number and in size throughout the world.

The French revolution, the Protestant reformation, the first and second world wars, the colonization of the third world nations, and the pangs and pains of the slave trade all contributed to the cultural and spiritual revolution of the church in the East and West, causing heretics and false witnesses to abound in the Christian world. In our present age, with the ecumenical agenda introduced by the Second Vatican Council (cf., *Unitatis redintegratio*), the church explains that it has always faced the problem of false witnesses even among the old and traditional churches of the West plus the young and vulnerable churches in Asia and Africa. This time, the issues are subtle and problematic. Joseph Cardinal Ratzinger (*Introduction to Christianity*, p. 41), focusing on the concept of belief in the world today and giving his fair assessment of the situation, writes,

> In the specific conditions of our modern situation, that belief or faith is problematical, indeed almost something that seems impossible, but that it has always meant a leap, a somewhat less obvious and less easily recognizable one perhaps across an infinite gulf, a leap namely out of the tangible world that presses man from every side.
>
> Belief has always had something of an adventurous break or leap about it because at every age it represents the risky enterprise of accepting what plainly cannot be seen as truly real and fundamental. Belief was never simply the attitude automatically corresponding to the whole slant of human life; it has always been a decision calling on the depths of existence, a decision that in every age demanded a turnabout by man that can only be achieved by an effort of will.

The Early Christian community that Jesus left were men and women of faith who lived out their faith in their lives because they knew in whom they believed – Jesus of Nazareth crucified, died, and resurrected. They turned themselves toward Jesus, and Him alone. But as to what is the meaning of faith or belief in our present generation, Ratzinger again laments,

> Belief appears no longer as the bold but challenging out of the apparent all our visible world and into the apparent void of the invisible and intangible; it looks much more like a demand to bind oneself to yesterday and to affirm it as eternally valid. And who wants to do that in an age when the idea of "tradition" has been replaced by the idea of "progress"?
>
> The Early Christian community left a "tradition", and that Tradition was faith in Jesus of Nazareth. Scripture and tradition were one coin of opposite sides. The Church especially the Catholic Church throughout the centuries relied on this tradition, guided it, and defended it, but again today "tradition appears to be what has been laid aside, the merely out of date, whereas progress is regarded as the real promise of life, so that man feels at home, not in the realm of tradition, of the past

> but in the realm of progress and the future. (p. 51-53)

This rupture between the old and new, between tradition and progress is part of the problem we as a church are currently facing.

Chapter 3
Bearing Witness
by Evangelizing the Cultures

Part of bearing witness to the Gospel is the renewal of the missionary spirit of the church through the process of evangelization of all cultures (see *Gaudium et space,* § 53.) Jesus was of his culture. He was a Jew by blood and grew up as one of the members of the Jewish community. He was so much at home with his culture that his first miracle at Cana was to change water into wine, just to provide service and care for his people. He visited the temple often and one day chased out the bad guys who were profiteering from the temple trade, using the house of God to make money. He observed their laws. He criticized the professionals of religion of his time, namely the scribes and pharisees who were strict observers of the Jewish tradition. His food, wares, and disciples were all Jewish. His mother and foster Father were Jewish.

But He was also against His culture by pointing out to His audience that they should remember what was said of old "an eye for an eye and a tooth for a tooth," but I say to you, "offer no resistance to one who is evil. When someone strikes you on your right cheek, turn the other one to him also" (Matthew 5:39). He taught and made radical changes to the law of Moses, but He said He had come to fulfill the law and the prophets, and He did.

He touched on the spirit of the law and condemned the outward observances of the law. He spoke about the root cause of anger and how it should be handled in the family. He taught about adultery and how important fidelity to one's marriage vows can support the unity of marriage. He taught about divorce, the taking of false oaths, issues of retaliation in society, and so on, but most importantly He made an important remark unheard of from any religion:

> "You have heard that it was said, You shall love your neighbor and hate your enemy, But I say to you, love your enemies and pray for those who persecute you, that you may be children of your heavenly Father for he makes his sun rise on the bad and good, and causes

rain to fall on the just and the unjust." (Matthew 5:43-48)

A Christian must go the extra mile to show love to his family, friends, neighbors, and enemies. This was a novelty he brought to Christianity. Jesus was also above his culture because He is God. "Whoever has seen me has seen the father. I and Father are one" (John 12:45). Evangelizing cultures means following these basic principles shown by Jesus himself while he was historically on earth.

Jesus was the first missionary! He was sent by the Father. He revealed the Father to the world. He also sent the advocate—the Holy Spirit to empower the church to be missionary. Essentially, the church is missionary, and missionary means we are sent to accomplish a specific task in a specific location using the same yard stick that Jesus used while on earth.

Applying these three principles, which I believe are at the heart of Christology, namely "Jesus and his culture, Jesus against his culture, and Jesus above his culture," the church is left with no other choice of approach to evangelization in our modern world. Cognizant of this approach, the Second Vatican

Council (1963-1965) gave a powerful testimony of the relationship between man and his culture in the world today.

Gaudium et spes (§53) states, "It is the characteristic of man that he cannot achieve true and full humanity except through culture, that is by cultivating natural resources and spiritual values. Wherever human life is involved, then nature and culture are closely connected." It goes further to define culture as:

> Everything by which man develops and refines his various gifts of mind and body. We speak of culture when ever he devotes himself to subduing the world to his control by knowledge and labor; when he humanizes social life on the family scale and on the civic by the progress of manners and institutions; lastly when in the course of time he expresses in his own achievements, great spiritual experiences and aspirations, communicating and preserving them so that they may profit many, even the whole human race.

In this context, therefore, each person and each culture must guide and protect the "natural resources and spiritual values" which are in indeed "loci" of evangelization. What must be evangelized first and foremost is the human person and secondly his culture. People of our own generation, especially in the developed countries, give more credence to natural resources than they give to spiritual values. Because of this imbalance of the assessment of culture, there are obvious reasons to believe among Christians that there must be a turn around to the center of gravity, which is God, not self, not the world nor to the devil.

The good news is that the United States Conference of Catholic Bishops has provided a wonderful road map by which the process of evangelizing cultures should proceed. In their document entitled "Go and make disciples," they gave three objectives to be accomplished namely,

> To bring about in all Catholics such an enthusiasm for their faith that in living their faith in Jesus, they freely share it with others; To invite all people in the United States whatever their social or cultural background, to hear the

message of salvation in Jesus Christ so they may come to join us in the fullness of the Catholic faith. To foster gospel values in our society, promoting the dignity of the human person, the importance of the family, and the common good of our society, so that our nation may continue to be transformed by the saving power of Jesus Christ.

To implement these objectives, they were able to identify those values that are good and should be shared and communicated to the whole world and the bad elements of the American cultures that need to be transformed by the gospel and worked upon by individual Christians. On the positive side of these values are "instinctual religiousness, its prizing of freedom and religious liberty, its openness to new immigrants and its inspiring idealism." On the negative side are "[m]aterialism, sexism, racism, consumerism, ... individualism run wild, ... [an] ethic of selfishness, ... [an] ignoring of the poor and weak, ... [a] disregard of human life and ... [the] endless chase of empty fads and immediate pleasures" (cf. Pelzel and Walters, *Ecclesiology*, pp. 77-84).

In my personal assessment of these values, whether negative or positive, I must confess as an immigrant from Nigeria that those of us who have lived here more than twenty years have cause to believe that most Americans, especially Catholics, are deeply religious, and the world is impacted by what happens here, the good, bad, or ugly. I never believed in my life that I would be a missionary in the United States. My native country was colonized by the British and Christianized by the Irish Missionaries. The early missionaries in Nigeria changed the culture of the people by changing their names, languages, and faith in their traditional religion. You need only read Chinua Achebe's *Things Fall Apart* to understand the extent of the damage done by the missionaries. But in the end, they left a vibrant church and a hope within the universal church for the future. It is not the case here in the United States. I feel the air of freedom and religious liberty here more pronounced than in my own country where there is still rivalry among Christians of different denominations.

Practicing Christianity where there is formidable competition among Islam, Christianity, and traditional religions can be very challenging. The danger of these amalgams of religious faith in my country is that they lead to syncretism and religious persecutions. Another example is the Middle East, where you have three major revealed religions trying to live together.

It seems to me that the American society is the ideal when it comes to religious freedom and liberty, but this is not to say it is perfect. After all, there are differences among Christian Churches in America, especially among non-Catholic Black and Hispanic churches. There is a general belief that America is open to immigrants, but immigration has been deeply politicized so much so that those who suffer much are immigrants themselves at the borders or at the US embassies abroad.

There is something exceptional about the American idealism that intrigues me, and that is the understanding that "nobody is above the law." This is why many countries all over the world cherish the American democracy. Pope Francis says, "There is no perfect society, no perfect man, no perfect family." So, as well, there is no perfect country, but some are more organized than others, and that is why corruption is minimized because of the enforcement of the rule of law. Again, people who are not US citizens may not realize that in the midst of religious liberty and freedom, you can be what you want to be, behave the way you want to behave, and grow up within whatever city, but when it comes to public office and you are seeking to be elected, then, you will be scrutinized inside out.

The message is that "our best must rule us," not the richest, or most powerful, or most well connected. America stands out in this area. Another area of interest is the nationalistic spirit among citizens. Catholics and non-Catholics, believers and non-believers are proud of their families of origin, their states of origin, and their country overall. America has nothing to do with ethnicity, but Americans have problems with racism and the socio-economic status of minorities. Consumerism is sometimes exaggerated, but the event of Covid-19 has shown that food can be scarce sometimes. It took time before the Covid vaccine reached everybody. Many lives were lost during Covid days, and continue to be lost to this date, but without the American ingenuity and fast intervention in the discovery of the vaccine, many more lives would have been lost.

Individualism and selfishness are twin vices learned by most European cultures where major discoveries have placed people on a high pedestal. There is and ego-complex here which needs to be addressed by individual Christians themselves by adhering to the much more Christian values of humility because, after all, what we are and what we have come from is God. Individualism and selfishness are universal vices spread all over the world, especially the civilized world where there are many narcissistic individuals who cannot live outside themselves.

My major concern is the area of relativizing the truth through ideologies. America is ideologically divided into right, left, and center, and each group holds fast to their ideology or program as the ultimate solution to human needs. The victims of this division are the ordinary citizens who do not understand the philosophy behind conservatism as opposed to liberalism. An example is necessary here. When it comes to the protection of life and property, the American spirit of the law will pursue its citizens' protection, and when it comes to the issues of Abortion rights, while some would argue that it is the right of the woman to decide what happens to the body, the pro-life group will argue that the unborn in the womb have rights, too, and must be protected. The "fight" between the pro-life and pro-choice is still on even with the Supreme Court's overturning of *Roe vs Wade* (1973). The issue of capital punishment is related to the issue of abortion since the bible said, "Thou shall not kill." Those waiting to be sent to death by this policy have a right to live. In other words, there is a dilemma as to which ideology is right or wrong and what is objectively true in all cases. Examples like these lead us to the problem of relativism.

To sum up this area of evangelizing the culture, I will affirm that the church in America, especially the Catholic Church where I belong and offer my ministry, is a fast-growing healthy church with the spirit of "koinonia" among the college of bishops. Most importantly, the clergy are happy with the work they are doing. Fr. Rossetti has published a new book on the priesthood dealing statistically with the mental health of the clergy. He wrote, "Almost universally, whether the priests were happy or not, I admired their self-sacrificing dedication to helping the people of God."

Chapter 4
Unfinished Business of Inculturation in the Church Universal

There are, of course, some issues of common concern which need to be enculturated into the church's way of life. In this section, I will examine them as pending topics being handled by the magisterium.

The German Catholic Church has raised the issue of allowing married and divorced faithful to receive communion. While some favored the idea, some ignored it as non-issue. But it is a major concern of churches in Germany. There are many faithful people who have been separated from their spouses for a long time and have entered into unions with others. They yearn to go back to church and continue to live their normal lives, but because their marriages were not annulled, they cannot receive communion.

Sexual abuse by priests and religious has caused unprecedented harm to the image and credibility of the church in our time. While some churches have come out with policies to this effect, it does appear that many churches in Latin America and Africa are yet to establish safe environment guidelines with regular checks and balances to protect both the priests and the victims. Is it not possible for the church to consider this topic as a cause for another synod or Ecumenical council? There must be a universal norm guiding the rights of victims and priests and religious working under them.

Sexual misconduct has permeated ecclesial ministry to the point where the minister is no longer trusted as a carrier of holy things. This occurs not only in our Catholic Church, but as a universal phenomenon. Meanwhile, there must be ongoing formation of priests and religious with an emphasis on the priestly virtues of chastity, celibacy, and pastoral charity. In any abuse, the priests and the victims are both wounded. Healing takes a long time, and both parties are in need of redemption.

The implementation of the "apostolate of the laity" (*Apostolicam actuositatem*) must broaden to include their involvement in the governance of the church. Pope Francis has brought this agenda to the limelight by appointing women with voting rights into the synodal hall. When the Germans introduced altar girls, some people frowned at it, but

Ch. 4: Unfinished Business of Inculturation

today it has become the order of the day. The German Church and USCCB are ahead of others in the involvement of the laity, but I would suggest further that the financial affairs of the parishes and dioceses be handled by competent lay faithful. "The love of money," 1 Timothy 6:10 explains, "is the root of all evil."

Language has been a powerful means of communication. The Second Vatican Council allowed the use of the vernacular to bring the gospel message home to the people. But I have discovered that the more languages you know, the more you are able to minister to many people. I am a beneficiary of the languages I can speak (Spanish, Italian, English), so I encourage ministers of the word to study other languages other than their own. I am particularly thinking about speaking dialects in my country other than Igbo language. How I wish I could speak Yoruba, or Hausa? Latin has been traditionally regarded as the universal language of the church. It would be a novelty to re-introduce Latin as the language of study in all the seminaries in the world to foster the unity of the universal Church and the international communication tool. Language has changed the way people worship with deep understanding of the word of God, but the people of God must be united in what I term the universal language of the Church. The ancient traditional Latin songs like "Ave Maris Stella," "Anima Christi," and "Sub tum Presidium" are beautiful hymns that call back memories of the ancient church.

Inter-religious dialogue has its merits and demerits. It has brought to the limelight the interconnectivity of all world religions and belief systems. It shows exactly those who believe in a supreme being and those who believe is an external force other than those who worship him. It demonstrated Judaism, Islam, and Christianity as three revealed religions whose founders lived historically here on earth. It connects us with the world and the needs of the world from religious persecution to the human rights abuses of all scales. It makes clear our differences and opens further areas of dialogue and understanding. On the demerit side, dialogue means "talk of equals" but it seems to me that revealed religions are more organized than natural or traditional religions. It seems to me that some religions are more belligerent than others. It seems to me that some are more peaceful and more inclusive than others, and what makes Christianity special is that it

Ch. 4: Unfinished Business of Inculturation 33

can abide and endure in any culture. Then I am asking out of curiosity these questions:

> Whoever would have believed that after the Second Vatican Council 1963-1965, there would be a change in approach in addressing the faith-based differences through what the Church calls today "inter-religious dialogue"? The council for inter-religious dialogue came into existence in 1985 with Francis Cardinal Arinze as the head during the Pontificate of Pope John Paul II. Are there tangible results of this dialogue or do we have multiplication of faith-based Christianity in the world?

> Whoever would have believed that the concern of the church today would be focused on how "to govern well" (Synodality) and not how "to define the articles of faith"? It is surprising how things have changed and how the wider spread of the gospels has also created new ways of church governance.

Angelo Cardinal Scola summarized the vision and mission of the church in the document *Gau-*

dium et Spes by stating that "two elements - a vision of man as related to Jesus Christ and an emphasis on the salvific - sacramental mission of the Church are the basis of the attitude of dialogue and discernment which the Church maintains towards the world in order to bear testimony to the truth."

"Eritis mihi testes" – What does it mean for the Christian community at our present generation? It means that to believe now is more difficult, it means that the "traditions" given to us by the early church are substituted with "progress". It means that to evangelize now means a total conversion of self, of culture, and of the world so that God can be brought back to the world as the center of gravity.

Chapter 5
False Witnesses Today

However, in our own time, there are evidently, witnesses to the faith who are fake, false, fickle, and ultimately weak to the point that their messages and persons drag their followers away from the orthodox churches to an independent and so-called free church. At what point can this multiplication of churches be stopped? The answer can only be guessed or left in the hands of providence. There are false witnesses in all denominations, but I would like to single out the developing nations in Africa and Latin America. (You only need to google to find out the rise and fall of most of these mega churches and their pastors. You only need to search these mega churches all over the world and see how they were founded and when they are closed for services to the public.)

In recent years especially in the African continent where Christianity is beginning afresh, there are so many **false witnesses**. When a church is turned into a business center, and the members believe that they will gain in that business through

prosperity messages and miracles will happen all the time, suppose, one miracle fails, as it does sometimes, the whole house crumbles to ashes. (The cases of pre-arranged miracles are the topic of the day in some devotional centers in my country Nigeria.)

There are many prosperity preachers, tele-evangelists, and self-ordained pastors, who have thrived in their ministry because they depended on giving hope to the hopeless and fickle-minded faithful who are vulnerable to succumb to the current gimmicks of false prophets and their co-disciples who have assumed the power to ordain ministers. The ministry of hope and sometimes despair is what is currently in vogue now, and sometimes the salvific value of sacrifice, the cross, the pain, the discipline, and the virtue of poverty is forgotten in their preaching.

A minister who preaches prosperity without the cross, and suffering of Jesus of Nazareth is a false witness to the gospel. A church that encourages those kinds of ministry and allows it to spread is either a false church or a secular business center. There were false prophets in the Old Testament, especially the prophets of Baal. The people knew them by their actions and their words. By "their fruits you shall know them" (Matt. 7:16). Many people who are parading themselves as the prophets of God are not real prophets but fortune tellers or prosperity preachers. Houses that have been turned into churches abound in many cities in West Africa, but these are business centers in the real sense of the term. What will happen when the so-called prophets are dead? Their patrimony will die with them because they have nothing to transfer of salvific value to the next generation.

Fake witnesses abound today in the name of Christianity. Most of these fake pastors take undue advantage of the poor and vulnerable people to confuse and mesmerize them to believe that their so-called miracles will work all the time. They fall prey to these pastors and lives are destroyed forever. Because most of the people have **weak** and **fickle faith**, and as long as they remain gullible to the things of the world, they will have the smallest resistance to temptation.

The current trend of Christianity of some of these "free churches" especially in the developing world like Africa, is a combination of syncretistic mix with African traditional religion. The current trend of Christianity in Europe, however, is the weakening of the Christian tradition, the loss of the sense of the sacred, and gradual denial of God's presence in the world. This is an after-effect of secularization which has metamorphosed into secularism. Few people, especially the old people in Europe, form most of the practicing Christians. They go to church regularly. The younger generations, many of them, have lost their trust in any form of religion. They hardly go to Church. This trend would endure unless something happens in terms of the new evangelization. The current trend of Christianity in America is the amalgam of the Latin American Christian surge of their own Christian faith with the dwindling faith of most American Christians. There is the atmosphere of relative attitude to the Christian faith and/or selection from the church laws, what people like and do not like in terms of Christian faith.

The major concern today is the crisis of relativism—an attitude where the objective truth is doubted or denied. The hope is that with intensified witness to the truth of Christianity by living authentic Christian lives as Jesus lived, dying with him as

Ch. 5: False Witnesses Today

he did, and sacrificing one's life as Jesus did, and perhaps adopting the true theology of the cross as the way to redeem the world, it would be very hard to equate the Christianity of the Apostolic times with the Christianity of the present generation. "To whom shall we go Lord" (John 6:68). This was the crucial question that Peter asked Jesus during his personal crisis. "You are the source of eternal life." We have no place to go or escape except to rely on the unfailing word of the Lord. "Heaven and Earth will pass away, but my word will not pass away" (Matt 24:35).

Thus, our prayer is summed up by saying, "Our help is in the name of the Lord, who made heaven and Earth." The consolation to what is happening today is that Jesus of Nazareth experienced the same kinds of false and fake witnesses in his own time. He spent a lot of time confronting the false teachers of the law, the scribes and the pharisees, and condemned their hypocrisy. He called them names, like "brood of vipers" (Matt. 12:34). He cursed them out. "Woe to you scribes and pharisees" (Matt. 23:13). They never changed their minds set in finding a way to kill him. They succeeded in killing him, but he rose from the dead. This journey that Jesus made should be the same journey the body of Christ – the Church – should make.

Chapter 6
Recommendations

I believe the church should condemn corruption of all kinds in government and in society, especially when the ordinary person in the street is denied basic human rights and dignity.

The church should also condemn false prophets and teachers who extort money from the faithful by preaching false prophecy and teaching false doctrines to the people.

The church should call a sin by its name and condemn it without further interpretation by the legal courts.

The mission of the church is to take care of the marginalized, the sick, the poor among us, the disabled, and the homeless. The primary job of the church is to "evangelize" and not to "civilize."

A church that is not ready to carry the cross of persecution in the areas where there is institutionalized injustice, prejudice, racial hatred, economic inequality, and ethnic or religious bigotry, is not bearing witness to the gospel.

A church that has no vision and mission for the future, no missionary intention to immediately touch lives of people is not bearing witness to the gospel.

What would be the church of our dreams? A church that is like the first Christian community—authentic, credible, reasonable, truthful, knowledgeable, faithful to the original faith, and responsible to the signs of our time.

It was St. Oscar Romero who once said, "A church that does not provoke any crisis, a gospel that doesn't unsettle, a word of God that doesn't get under anyone's skin, a word of God that doesn't touch the real sin of the society in which it is being proclaimed…. what kind of gospel is that"?

It is generally believed by Catholics that the bishops represent the apostles, and that the Pope is the head of the college of Bishops. Among the early apostles, some were very close to their master. One of them (Judas) was a traitor, Thomas doubted about the risen Lord, Peter denied his master three times, but beside their individual personalities, they had unity of purpose, that is, to proclaim Jesus' death and resurrection. They gave up their lives in defense of this enduring truth.

What, if an individual bishop fails to bear witness to the risen Lord by failing to maintain collegial collaboration with fellow bishops and does his own thing in isolation of the magisterium?

What if the priests who are close collaborators of the bishops decide to live as loners and do things against the minds of the church (*contra mentem Ecclesiae*). Are they bearing witness to the risen Lord?

The second Vatican Council emphasized the role of the laity in the church. By virtue of one's baptism, the faithful are invited to holiness and to participate actively in bearing witness to the gospel. The faithful who are indifferent to the teachings of the Church and try to trivialize the doctrines as outdated information are not bearing witness to the gospel.

Yes, some may say, we have one God, but not all religions are the same. Some religions are more organized than others. Some religions are more peaceful than others. While some religions are more belligerent than others, some are more tolerant, more ecumenical, and more inclusive. It is dangerous to assume that all religions are the same. They are not. Christianity is different from Islam and Judaism. But Islam is different from Buddhism. Buddhism is different from African Traditional religions. What is important is that you must practice what you preach and teach what you preach to your members in faith and honesty so that it can impact your own life and those around you. The love of God and neighbor enshrined in the holy book can be expressed differently in other religions, but Christianity goes beyond the other religions by emphasizing "Love your enemies" and "Do good to those who hate you" because God loves everybody, the good, the bad, and the ugly. He allows his sunshine on everyone. He allows the air we breathe to flourish in everyone. He allows the rain to fall on every soil and on everyone. He spreads the seasons to everyone according to their locations. As the psalmist would sing, "If God is for us who can be against us?" Jesus referred to his disciples as the "salt of the earth" or "light of the world." If the salt loses its taste, what use has it but to be thrown away. If the light is hidden under our private homes and beds, what use is the light to be called light?

The church stands to lose its vision and mission when it is no longer credible, truthful, responsible, and reasonable among the people and in the modern world today.

"I have a dream" that one day, the church and its members will return to the apostolic times when all Christians will be one in faith and in spirit and begin to love one another as the Early Christians did.

My humble recommendation is that the Catholic Church should revisit the documents of the second Vatican Council and have the policies articulated by the council fathers implemented, especially the doctrinal and liturgical constitutions (*Sacrosanctum Concilium, Lumen Gentium,*

Ch. 6: Recommendations

and *Dei Verbum*). It does seem to me that Vatican II documents have not permeated into the fabric of the Church universal.

With all the good and honest intentions of the Council Fathers, the ordinary people have not grasped well the depth and meaning of the church today. There remains to be done a lot of work on the catechesis of the teachings of the second Vatican Council to the ordinary folks throughout the world.

For clarity of purpose, I would like to cite the observation of Avery Cardinal Dulles in his book *Reshaping Catholicism* to buttress the fact that the documents of the Second Vatican Council have not been accepted or implemented fully.

> Vatican II has become, for many Catholics, a center of controversy. Some voices from the extreme right and extreme left frankly reject the council. Reactionaries of the traditionalist variety censure it for having yielded to Protestant and modernist tendencies. Radicals of the far left, conversely, complain that the council, while making some progress, failed to do away with the church's absolutistic claims and its antiquated class structure.

> The vast majority of Catholics, expressing satisfaction with the results of the council, are still divided because they interpret it in contrary ways. (p. 19)

And in another instance, he said,

> For them, Vatican II made a decisive break with the juridicism, clericalism, and triumphalism of recent centuries and laid the foundations for a more liberal and healthier Catholicism (idem). One can understand the efforts of our current Pope, to bring the "left", "the right", and the "center" together into one table of the Lord. He is bearing witness to the gospel by maintaining the principle of "inclusiveness" in the church just like Jesus did by dining with "sinners and tax collectors, by curing the lepers, restoring the blind to see, the deaf to hear, and the lame to work". This tension has been recurrent and ought to be taken as a daily cross to bear the witness of Christ crucified by all Christians all over the world.

Conclusion

I conclude this peace by saying that the church that is afraid to carry this "burden," the cross, this "tension of inclusiveness" even though it might not be a popular opinion, is running a risk of losing its members, of not being credible, of not being truthful and authentic. The early church was an inclusive church, and a divided church is a misnomer! How I wish our Churches would maintain this rhythm of love and truth throughout the earth. "Come Holy Spirit and fill the hearts of the faithful and enkindle in them the fire of your love" Amen.

Works Consulted or Referenced

Dulles, Cardinal Avery. *The Reshaping of Catholicism.* San Francisco: Harper & Row, 1988.

Dulles, Cardinal Avery. *The Craft of Theology.* New York: Crossroad, 1992.

Kelly, J.N.D. *Early Christian Doctrines.* New York: Harper & Row, 1978.

Komonchak, Joseph A. *Who are the Church?* Milwaukee, WI: Marquette University Press. 2008.

New American Bible. Winona, MN: St. Mary Press, 1991.

Pelzel, Morris, and Thomas P. Walters, eds. *Ecclesiology the Church as Communion. Catholic Basics. A Pastoral Ministry Series.* Chicago: Loyola Press, 2001.

Ratzinger, Cardinal Joseph. *Credo for Today: What Christians Believe.* San Francisco: Ignatius Press, 2009.

Ratzinger, Cardinal Joseph. *Introduction to Christianity.* San Francisco: Ignatius Press, 2004.

Rossetti, Msgr. Stephen J. *Priesthood in the time of crisis.* Notre Dame, Indiana: Ave Maria Press, 2023.

Vatican II Documents Referenced

Sacrosanctum concilium (December 4, 1963)
Unitatis redintegratio (November 21, 1964)
Lumen gentium (November 21, 1964)
Dei verbum (November 18, 1965)
Gaudium et spes (December 7, 1965)

www.ingramcontent.com/pod-product-compliance
Lightning Source LLC
Chambersburg PA
CBHW060355050426
42449CB00011B/3000